Joy in the Sorrow

Sara J. Hoffman

WESTBOW
PRESS®
A DIVISION OF THOMAS NELSON
& ZONDERVAN

WestBow Press books may be ordered through booksellers or by contacting:

WestBow Press
A Division of Thomas Nelson & Zondervan
1663 Liberty Drive
Bloomington, IN 47403
www.westbowpress.com
844-714-3454

ISBN: 978-1-6642-0707-3 (sc)
ISBN: 978-1-6642-0708-0 (e)

Library of Congress Control Number: 2020918717

Print information available on the last page.

WestBow Press rev. date: 10/29/2020

Contents

Preface

The Lord says, "I will guide you along the best pathway for your life. I will advise you and watch over you."

—Psalm 32:8

We must simply show up and be open to divine guidance, and it will always be there. I submit my will to God's to write this book. This is God's specific assignment and calling for me. We are blessed with the supernatural joy of following God. If we take the leap of faith in following what he is asking us to do, he will take care of the details and equip us with the resources we need to fulfill his purpose through us. British evangelist and author Smith Wigglesworth wrote, "God does not call those who are equipped; he equips those whom he has called."

Mark Twain said, "The two greatest days of your life are the day you were born and the day you find out why." Success has to do with obedience to God and doing things his way. God is sovereign and has power and all authority over all his creations to fulfill his will.

Faith is not about everything turning out okay; it is about being okay no matter how things turn out. Having faith, hope, and determination doesn't take away the feeling involved. Be kind to yourselves with whatever battles you are facing. Deep faith doesn't look picture-perfect. It is not simply sitting pretty in precarious situations, unfazed by it all. Instead, it is messy and sweaty and full of tears.

Faith is desperately grabbing on to God's hand while hanging off the edge of the cliff. It is feeling yourself slip but trusting that even if you fall, he will catch you. Faith is believing that the mountain you are hanging from, the ground hundreds of feet below, is actually a sturdy and stable stepping stone purposely placed there to draw you closer to the presence of God.

Faith brings hope in the aftermath, joy in the sorrow, steady in the chaos. All these and more are the proof that our anchors run deep, that the storms may swell, but we won't drown and that the eyes that have seen the unimaginable can be lifted up. For we constantly call out to the one who is able, and he sustains us for one more second to take one more step, all the way home.

Six or seven years ago, some great spiritual friends of ours, Nick and Christine, invited us to their small group, which focused on Rick Warren's *The Purpose Driven Life* (Zondervan 2002). Pastor Warren emphasized that God has created each and every one of us for his divine purpose.

When I took quiet time in prayer to ask God of his purpose for my life, he revealed it to me through the Holy Spirit. He said that it is his will and purpose for my life that I write a book sharing the great tapestry he wove during my brother, Matt's, struggle with brain cancer that ended in March of 2012. It is to rejoice in all the blessings surrounding this journey of a twenty-six-year-old battling brain cancer.

A special thanks to Lorna Pendell for revising and editing my work as well as her moral support throughout my writing journey.

Introduction

I took time after Matt's death to jot down all of the positive people, nature, and circumstances that blessed Matt and our entire family during this five-year journey. As a mother of three teens who are very active in school and sports activities, I put off God's calling and the purpose that he had spoken to me. In 2018, I finally completely surrendered to his will to write this book. God cleared my schedule in terms of my part-time job since there wasn't an active client for me at this time.

The year 2018 was one of pain and confusion for me. I feel like this dark time was to stir my need to grow closer to God. I know my healing involves spending time writing for his glory. This was confirmed through a sermon about pain that I heard.

Pain is transformative; it connects us. Strength does not connect us. Pain helps us relate to each other. Jesus can step into pain and use us. Pain is healing, a purpose, and a platform. I knew God was using this pain for his good purpose. I have learned, through my brother's death and the dark time I have recently gone through, that it's these times that draw us closer to God. Sometimes the bad things that happen in our lives put us directly on the path to the best things that will ever happen to us.

By being authentic with our pain and struggles, we can help others. Pain leads us closer to God, who is the only one who can truly fill us up in this life. We all try to fill ourselves with the things of this world, but we are spiritual beings who can only be truly filled with joy by God. God is unchanging, as is his love for us. Humans are sinners, and our sin nature causes us to disappoint, fail, and cause pain. God is the only constant we have in our lives. God is our strength and the only one who can heal broken hearts. A heart that is broken is a heart that is open.

This past year found me in the midst of a dark, emotional storm filled with confusion. Seven years ago I had been through a study about spiritual warfare, and I feel like Satan created a battle in my mind with my feelings, heart, and mind, all in confusion and contradicting one another. I have had to accept the fact that I can't know everything and that it isn't for me to figure out. He also used this heartbreak to ignite the purpose he has for me here on earth to write his book to give others hope in difficult times. He says that he uses our trials and suffering for his greater purpose.

On Facebook, Christine Caine wrote, "When you're in a dark place, you sometimes tend to think you've been buried, but perhaps you've been planted."

You can bloom.

The devil tried to spin me out of control and take me off course altogether. God sustained me, and the only way for me to stand against this warfare in my mind was to remember some of his promises and to be in prayer. God isn't a God of confusion but of peace.

"Be still and know that I am God" (Psalm 46:10).

- God is with you in the valleys, the tough times.
- God's got this. He is bigger than my enemies.
- God is concerned with what concerns you.
- Live in peace and trust God.
- An attitude of faith is what allows God to do amazing things.
- Don't allow yourself to be stuck in the past.
- If someone did you wrong, let it go and move on.
- See every circumstance and challenge as a blessing and not a curse.

- Win by focusing on your future.
- There is purpose in your pain.
- Keep being your best and let God fight your battles.
- People don't determine your destiny, God does.
- It is beautiful to be the instrument of God's world, wielding power to kill sin.

Whenever fear or craving lead us astray:

"I am with you always, even to the end of the age" (Matthew 28:20).

"And this same God who takes care of me will supply all your needs from his glorious riches, which have been given to us in Christ Jesus" (Philippians 4:19).

"Then call on me when you are in trouble and I will rescue you, and you will give me glory" (Psalm 50:15).

In the fall of 2018, God led me to study through the Bible study fellowship The People of the Promised Land Part 1. The Bible records the pain of broken relationships, betrayals, and tragic conflicts and the joys of loyalty, victories, and family. God uses imperfect people like you and me to accomplish his plans and purposes. Situations may shake us, but Jesus is present with his people. Through his word and spirit, we can see him walking with us in our struggles and our joys. God is faithful in healing broken hearts and is restoring mine by accomplishing his will for me by writing this book.

Also in the fall of 2018, I was invited to do a six-week Bible study called the Armor of God by Priscilla Shirer. God's timing was perfect with this study as it emphasized that for our struggle isn't against flesh and blood but against the rulers, against the powers, against the world forces of this darkness, against the spiritual forces of wickedness in the heavenly places. The effects of the war going on in the unseen world reveals itself in strained, damaged relationships, emotional instability, mental fatigue, and physical exhaustion. The one responsible for all this is the devil himself.

I felt these effects of my personal war this past year. I learned the enemy would like to keep you in a space of shame and guilt and trick you into thinking your situation will never change and that God doesn't hear you or care when you call out to him. Satan wants to break fellowship between you and God. The enemy wants to stop or delay the plans and purposes of God. The enemy's appearance is attractive, alluring, and charming. He places temptations in your path. He tries to tempt you toward certain sins and convince you that can tolerate them without risking consequences.

Prayer is the connective tissue between you and heavenly places. Satan wants to weaken the believer's confidence and influence by conveying condemnation and guilt. He will misconstrue the truths of your personal reality and circumstances. The enemy hopes you trust your feelings and will be directed by them instead of following the truth of God's word. We can't make decisions based on feelings because feelings change and are subject to external stimuli. Actions done in faith must be anchored in something more solid and fixed than feelings.

We need to be serious about our faith and prayer to conquer the enemy. We can't conquer him without plugging into God. God is a miracle worker; so stay strong through prayer and his word to safely bring you through. God is continually working out his perfect will for our lives.

Trust in the Lord with all your heart; do not depend on your own understanding.

—Proverbs 3:5

Many times in our lives, we wonder why something is happening or question the timing of its occurrence. The verse above says God sees the entire picture, so trust in his plans and purposes for our lives, even it doesn't make sense to you. This verse asks us to look less at ourselves and more at God.

My younger brother was diagnosed at the age of twenty-six with a brain tumor in August 2006. His life literally changed overnight. His girlfriend of only eight months witnessed him having a seizure in the middle of the night. Matt would have been unaware of the seizure if Melissa hadn't been there.

I felt my stomach drop when I heard this. Thoughts raced through my mind as to what could have caused the seizure—low blood sugar, epilepsy, a brain tumor. When my mom told me the doctors thought it was a brain tumor, I felt physically and mentally sick. The doctors wouldn't know for certain until they went in to remove some of the mass that was putting pressure on his brain.

I already had a trip booked for me and my children to visit my best friend, Sara, in Madison, Wisconsin. From Clarkston, Michigan, the trip would have us travel through Chicago, the city where Matt lived, on the same day Matt was scheduled to meet with the doctors to discuss the MRI results and to plan for a surgery date. I, of course, knew I was meant to stop in Chicago and be part of this appointment with my mother and brother. I was shocked at how large the tumor was and how it had the right hemisphere of the brain completely pushed over. The brain had just adjusted to make room for this large tumor, and the brain continued to function normally for so long.

I felt a lack of control knowing that something can be in our bodies killing us without our knowledge. We can go to the doctor for our physicals and be told that we are in good health because our bloodwork came back as normal, but meanwhile, we have some ticking time bomb in our brains or another part of our bodies.

Wait patiently for the Lord. Be brave and courageous. Yes, wait patiently for the Lord.

—Psalm 27:14

I felt that my timely trip to Madison was God's plan for two purposes. The first was to be there for Matt's appointment. Secondly, it was to reconnect with a friend from high school whose husband had been diagnosed with a brain tumor a couple of years previous. Stacey, a dear friend who I grew up with and was a bridesmaid in my wedding, lives in Madison. She had heard from her mom about Matt's recent diagnosis of a possible glioma brain tumor. We visited for a couple of hours. She had seen an article in her local paper featuring a family in Madison, Wisconsin, who heads up a nonprofit organization called Headrush.

That family was young, and the intent of their organization was to support a professorship for brain tumor research at the University of Wisconsin-Madison. Stacey handed me the article and said there is hope for my brother. The man mentioned in the article was a young father, and he was able to have children despite having brain cancer. I looked at the picture of the family and realized that I went to junior high and high school in Appleton, Wisconsin, with his wife. I was shocked to have made this connection at just the right time, made by God's hand.

I immediately got in contact with this friend, whom I hadn't spoken to for more than ten years. Brandi provided information on the subject of brain tumors and gave me comfort. Being Matt's oldest sister, I took on the responsibility to research and learn more about this subject that was so new and unfamiliar to my family. God sent Brandi to me as another angel of support, comfort, and knowledge. What a comfort to explore a scary illness with an unpredictable outcome with a friend who is more seasoned on the subject. I was comforted knowing that we could walk the road together in faith.

"Yes, I am the vine; you are the branches. Those who remain in me, and I in them, will produce much fruit. For apart from me you can do nothing" (John 15:5).

In a conversation on the phone with Sara, she mentioned a childhood friend of her family's and their daughter Kate. Kate had a tumor on her brain stem as a young child. I remembered this family since Sara and I have been friends since we were four years old and would swim at the country club pool with these younger kids. Kate was my brother's age. I told Sara I remembered Kate from Appleton, where we grew up. Sara told me that Kate's brain tumor was benign and she survived. She does have slight paralysis on one side of her smile as a side effect of the brain tumor.

I asked my brother if he knew of Kate from Appleton, and he said he knew her and that she lived near him in Chicago. She is good friends with the circle of Matt's close friends. God had sent another angel from above who walks with a daily reminder in her smile of the tumor on her brain stem. The love in her heart for others suffering from brain tumors was apparent to Matt and Melissa through her faithful friendship and help to them in Chicago.

"The Lord is my strength and song" (Exodus 15:2).

God's Word was my constant strength and companion throughout Matt's journey.

"For God loved the world so much that he gave his one and

only son, so that everyone who believes in him will not perish but have eternal life" (John 3:16).

"I am the resurrection and the life. Anyone who believes in me will live, even after dying" (John 11:25).

In September 2011, I was invited to Bible Study Fellowship (BSF) (International Bible Study) by a friend who moved to Michigan from California a few years ago. We studied the Acts of the Apostles. It gave me lessons on steps of assurance to share with Matt to ensure his salvation. This study also helped me accept and get through the death of Matt six months later. God's timing with this invitation to BSF was perfect for allowing me to have fellowship with Matt on important things as well as to grow my faith and impact my own immediate family. I am so thankful for God's timing and how he incorporated this into his eternal plan.

God had a plan for me to meet some wonderful women in BSF at just the right time. He sovereignly placed me in leader Erin's group. Erin lost her young sister-in-law to breast cancer just a few weeks before Matt died. Erin and I were able to share our emotions and fellowship over the decline and then loss of our loved ones. We shared so much and were able to comfort each other along the way.

February 19, 2012, I found out that Matt's cancer and second tumor were growing and that the chemo treatment wasn't working. The doctors were going to stop treatment, and Matt was given six to twelve weeks to live. I crossed paths with Erin while I was sitting in my car alone, sobbing over Matt's prognosis. I was in the parking lot of Stars and Stripes Gymnastics while both of my girls were at practice.

Erin was walking into the building to get a Barbie that her daughter's aunt, who had just passed away, had given them. They forgot it earlier when they were at camp. Erin said she doesn't ever go to Stars and Stripes, but her girls did a one-time camp there earlier in the day. Another example of God's perfect timing. Erin was able to comfort me and share in the pain of my news. Her heart had just experienced the same thing, so God knew she had a special place of understanding and compassion for me.

Another special friend God placed in my BSF group was Theresa. When Matt passed away, Theresa gave me a very special study bible that I still use. She mentioned in her sympathy card that Matt means "gift of the Lord." During Matt's burial, the priest asked if anyone knew the meaning of Matthew. I knew that Matthew meant "gift of the Lord" because of what Theresa had written.

"The Lord has made everything for his own purposes" (Proverbs 16:4). The priest said that Matt was the Lord's gift and that he is back with the Lord in peace and his spirit lives on.

"God will raise us from the dead by his power [resurrection] just as he raised our Lord from the dead" (1 Corinthians 6:14).

There was a young male teacher who was diagnosed with a brain tumor at the school where my mom was employed as a secretary. His diagnosis came just a couple of months after Matt's. He died around Christmastime, just two months before Matt's death. The entire staff at the school was so supportive and rallied for Matt and Steve during this difficult time. My mom also had the support of Steve's mom, sharing their experiences and feelings surrounding their sons' terminal illnesses and deaths.

My mom and Steve's were part of the brain tumor support group in the Fox Cities and were thankful for the comfort this group provided them through answers, information, and support. The staff at my mom's school did a brain tumor walk as a team in memory of Matt and Steve, forming a team and wearing a team shirt in the fight against cancer.

God again introduces friends and people to us at just the perfect time. He provides the support he knows we will need to get through rough times.

3

Love is patient and kind. Love is not jealous or
boastful or proud. Love never gives up, never
loses faith, is always hopeful, and endures through
every circumstance.

—1 Corinthians 13:4, 7

Matt's number-one angel sent by God through his journey
with brain cancer was his wife, Melissa. After he graduated
with a bachelor degree in accounting from University of Wisconsin-
Madison, Matt moved to Chicago to work for the firm Ernst and
Young. Melissa moved from Dayton, Ohio, to work for them as
well. The two met at a work Christmas party in December 2005.
Melissa was Matt's first true love, and we were able to meet her in
April when she joined him back in Wisconsin for Easter.

In August 2006, just eight short months after they began
dating, Melissa woke in the middle of the night to witness Matt
having the seizure. The seizure led Matt to the hospital for the
tests and scans that told of his worst nightmare: the seizure
was due to brain cancer. He was diagnosed after surgery at
Northwestern Hospital in Chicago with a grade III astrocytoma/
oligoastrocytoma brain tumor in the right frontal temporal area.

The surgeon removed 70 percent of Matt's tumor, but there
were finger-like tumors infiltrating the brain. The surgeon
compared this to spilling salt on the ground—you can clean up

salt, but you can never know that you got each and every granule. The same goes with the brain tumor; and if you missed one brain cancer cell, it could continue to grow. By removing it all, you would lose too many vital brain cells, which would cause physical and mental impairments.

When Matt was undergoing brain surgery, I remember thinking, *I wonder what Melissa will do.* She was Matt's girlfriend for only eight months, and it would be easy for her to walk away from this, a situation that was too much to handle for most people in their twenties. It broke my heart to think that Matt may lose her during this sad and depressing time in his life. I wouldn't have blamed her for walking away, though. I think many people would have walked away to protect themselves from the hurt and pain. Melissa decided to stay since her love for Matt was so true.

Her being in Chicago with Matt was such a comfort for our entire family as my mom lives in Appleton, Wisconsin; my dad is in Appleton; I live in Clarkston, Michigan, and my sister lives in Baltimore, Maryland. Melissa's mom came to support our family over the weekend of Matt's surgery in Chicago, and she supported Matt and his relationship with Melissa. We all felt truly blessed to have these people we barely knew be with us, and their care and love for Matt surrounded us at one of the most difficult times of our lives. I believe God specifically sent Melissa into Matt's life to be his angel caregiver and allow Matt to experience his love of a lifetime. Falling in love would be one of the best ways God could comfort Matt and all of us during the course of his terminal illness.

Melissa married Matt on July 11, 2009. She was a faithful friend and wife to Matt during his last five years and seven months on this earth. God knew Melissa would stick with him through this difficult process. God sent her as part of his plan and purpose for Matt's life. God had a plan and knew Melissa's strong, steadfast love for Matt would pull her through. Thank you, dear God, for the greatest blessing of Melissa that you sent to Matt and our entire family.

Share each other's burdens, and in this way obey
the law of Christ.

—Galatians 6:2

Christians are meant to help each other with the loads they carry when they become overwhelming. We are called to be there for one another.

A couple friends came into my life during Matt's journey. One was a dear friend I spent many years with while both my girls did competitive gymnastics with both of her girls. Our girls were on the same teams, so we spent lots of time together during competitions, while carpooling, and other events. Kelly was a nurse for a neurosurgeon, so she dealt daily with many people who had glioma brain cancer, just like my brother. She knew all about the prognosis, the mystery, and the path specific for each patient. She and I conversed often on this subject.

I dropped my daughter's friend Kaelyn at her home after she and my daughter Molly did a gymnastics class together. I was outside talking to Kaelyn's parents when one of their neighbors, who I recognized from a gym class, walked by. In a matter of five minutes of conversation, we came to the knowledge that we were both affected by a loved one with a glioma brain tumor. Laura's mom passed away of glioblastoma when Laura was in her early twenties.

Since Laura and I recognized each other from a gym class, we talked about exercise and what classes we had been attending. We both mentioned we were running outside quite a bit to train for some races. I was training for the Crim, and she said that she was doing a run for a young girl who passed away of brain cancer. This is how we came to learn that we had a brain cancer diagnosis in both of our families. Another person I could share with. I ended up running the AdvoKate race with Laura since I loved the cause and it would be good preparation for the Crim.

AdvoKate is a volunteer organization established in honor of a six-year-old Kate Hrischuk of Rochester, Michigan, who lost her life to an intrinsic brain stem glioma in early 2007. AdvoKate supports the fight against childhood brain tumors at St. Jude Children's Research Hospital in Memphis, Tennessee, one of the nation's most trusted charities.

5

Keep on asking, and you will receive what you ask for. Keep on seeking, and you will find. Keep on knocking, and the door will be opened to you.

—Matthew 7:7

My prayer was for Matt to pass quickly and not suffer long. My prayer was that he would pass while we were all together in Chicago over the weekend. Matt was only different from his normal self for three months before he died, otherwise he walked around for most of his life with what appeared to be total health.

In February 2012, about a month before Matt died, my daughter Kaitlyn attended her friend Brooke's birthday party. At the drop-off, Brooke's mom, Heather, asked how I'd been. I told her my brother, who had brain cancer, was going downhill and that I had been traveling to Chicago off and on to see him. She told me that she would be going to Chicago on March 8 for a mom-to-mom sale that she does every year with her cousin there. Heather said she would be leaving on that Thursday by herself to drive to Chicago and that I was more than welcome to ride with her. I told her it would be unlikely that I would join her, as a week or two before we would be going to Chicago as a family for midwinter break. I knew Melissa didn't want constant visitors.

A day after we returned from our midwinter break visit, I

got a call from my mom saying that Matt had gone downhill and that they were going to stop all treatments, including steroids, chemotherapy, and radiation. I called Heather and decided to take her up on the offer for a ride to see Matt again since I knew he probably only had a few months to live. I believe that at that time they gave him six to twelve weeks. It wasn't easy as my kids, who were in fifth, third, and first grades, didn't have school that Friday, so I had to make arrangements for friends to help me out watching the kids.

I arrived around 9:00 or 10:00 p.m. in Chicago with Heather. Matt was bedridden as he'd had a breakthrough seizure that weakened him after being taken off his steroids. Matt opened his eyes and saw me when I arrived, but then his breathing got heavy and sounded very labored to me. Mom had just been there the previous day and hadn't mentioned anything about this. Matt wasn't able to speak to me and closed his eyes shortly after. He never opened them again and seemed to be in a coma. Hospice had been there the previous day and said Matt was doing well and showing no signs of dying soon. I talked to Mom again on Friday and told her of Matt's breathing.

Melissa's mom and grandma happened to be visiting that weekend from Ohio. Melissa's mom is a nurse and was concerned with Matt's breathing, but she said that this type of breathing could go on for weeks. She witnessed this before her dad passed away. Mom called me around noon and said that she'd decided to come to Chicago to be with us since she just had a feeling she should be there.

As soon as she said that she was planning to travel from Appleton, Wisconsin, to Chicago, Matt's breathing went from labored sounding to completely normal for the entire duration of her trip. I almost called my mom to tell her to hold off from coming. It was amazing since it began to labor again three and a half hours later, as soon as my mom arrived at Matt's doorstep.

It was like Matt waited peacefully for her to arrive and knew she was on her way.

Soon after, we told Matt that it would be okay to let go and that we would all be okay and so would he. I called my sister, grandma, my husband, Kris, and my dad, and they were all able to say their goodbyes to Matt over the phone. Melissa had a futon set by his bedside, and she turned the lights off and lay down to hear what she thought was Matt's breathing returning to the normal it had been earlier that day. Around 10:00 p.m., when we all lay down to sleep, Matt passed away.

As soon as she turned the light back on, she discovered he had let go and fallen into the eternal life of Jesus Christ, another part of God's perfect plan by naturally adjoining people from three different states to be together to support Melissa and one another during this difficult time. God used a friend near me to carry out his perfect plan in his perfect timing. Now that is a God who proves to be in control of everything.

You saw me before I was born. Every day of my life was recorded in your book. Every moment was laid out before a single day had passed.

—Psalm 139:16

For we know that when this earthly tent we live in is taken down (that is, when we die and leave this earthly body), we will have a house in heaven, an eternal body made for us by God himself and not by human hands.

—2 Corinthians 5:1

Our life on earth is preparation for our eternal life. Our earthly life is but a blip in time compared to that of eternity. Matt passed away on our stepfather's birthday, March 9, 2012. He was blessed in that he was fully himself without any impairments until just three months before he died. His short-term memory became affected around Thanksgiving 2011. It slowly worsened. My mom planned a final trip for Matt, my son, and my husband to fly out to California for the Wisconsin Badger Rose Bowl game. My Mom decided to go along to help Matt with the transfer flights at the airport as we didn't trust his memory enough to be confident he wouldn't get lost. It was a wonderful trip for all, and the memories will last a lifetime. They had left near my son, Kristoffer's, eleventh birthday.

Matt's funeral was held on March 13, 2012, which is my dad's birthday. Matt was cremated, and his burial was in the spring in May on my birthday. That was the date that worked for everyone coming from Ohio, Illinois, Michigan, and Wisconsin to meet in Appleton, Wisconsin for the burial. It was no coincidence that all these important dates were birthdates within our family.

The priest presiding over Matt's burial said that the fact that the passing and celebrations surrounding it landed on family birthdays represented Matt beginning his new life in heaven— that he is born again into heaven.

7

Be still and know that I am God.

—Psalm 46:10

K nowing God results in every other kind of understanding
We see signs and look back, and things now make sense to us.

On Matt's May burial date, God gave us a couple of signs to show us that he and Matt's spirit were with us! First, Kris grabbed his phone out of the car as we were stepping out to walk to Matt's burial site. A photo of Matt and our son, Kristoffer, from their final trip to the Rose Bowl, appeared on his screen. This photo randomly appeared without him trying to bring up photos. This had never happened to Kris before, so he was amazed by this sign.

After Matthew was buried, everyone stepped away. I spent a few moments at Matt's gravesite because I knew I wouldn't be back from Michigan very often to visit it. A bright red cardinal flew and swooped down right in front of Matt's grave. The Holy Spirit immediately said to me that that is a sign from Matt. The bright red color reminded me of Matt's love for the Wisconsin Badger red, being that my sister, brother, and I, as well as my husband and his twin brothers graduated from the University of Wisconsin-Madison. We are all very faithful Badger fans, even though none of us currently reside in the state of Wisconsin. I also felt in my heart that this was a sign for Matt as his last big trip before his death was to see Wisconsin play in the Rose Bowl.

I would see cardinals often from time to time after Matt passed away. One evening, a few weeks before Christmas, I pulled into my driveway and was talking on the phone with my mom. I wasn't able to pull all the way into the garage as we had our boat there for the winter. I pulled in at an angle, and my headlights shined on the white house. As we were finishing up our conversation, I thought I saw something red on the branch of our tree. I thought, *This can't possibly be a cardinal.* I had never seen a bird at night sitting still on a tree.

I got out of the car and walked over to the tree; and sure enough, it was a cardinal. I was able to get a foot away from it, and it didn't move. I could not believe it. It was just a couple of feet away from our garage door and the house lights nearby. It ended up coming to that same spot every night until this first Christmas, where Matt had not spent it here on earth. Every night, my garage door would go up and down several times with the comings and goings of my girls' gymnastics practices and my son's basketball practices. The cardinal would still come and wasn't scared by our activity or our approaching it.

It was clear to me this was a sign from God that my brother is all right and that there is more beyond this earth to clue us in to heaven if we are still and notice God's signs. I would show this amazing sign of the cardinal to anyone who came to our door in the evening. Any visitor who came to the house during this three-week period witnessed this miraculous sign. I took a picture of the cardinal and sent it out on Facebook, saying I wished everyone faith that holiday season and that this cardinal is a sign of faith to me.

My friend Santina commented on my post, saying if you Google what a cardinal represents, you will see that it is a sign of the afterlife. Its red color represents the blood of Jesus Christ shed for the redemption of mankind. The bird's name, cardinal, is actually derived from the royal red vestments worn by Catholic cardinals, the hierarchy of the church. The cardinal symbolizes hope, joy, health, rejuvenation, and celebration, especially to the ones who look beyond in searching their meaning.

A red cardinal has long been held as the most notable spiritual messenger. When it comes to you almost insistently trying to gain your attention, it is likely you are receiving a message from spirit. The red cardinal comes in the winter season of one's life to bring the reminder that the blood of Jesus takes away all our sins and makes us as white as the freshly fallen snow, with no mistakes left showing. The red symbolizes God's forgiveness showing him to be the great redeemer—redeeming trash into treasure, which is his life inside us.

I just couldn't believe what I had learned about the cardinal when I researched its meaning. I was in awe of how God uses nature as a sign from heaven. I was at complete peace knowing God had a perfect plan for Matt's life and that he was using the cardinal as a reassurance to speak this to me. Oh, how great God is and loves us all so much to show up in such a meaningful and purposeful way.

"But in fact, it is best for you that I go away, because if I don't, the Advocate won't come. If I do go away, then I will send him to you" (John 16:7).

The Holy Spirit was telling me the cardinal is the sign of Matthew and the Holy Spirit was nudging me to tell my story to others. When God shows up in a tangible, surprising way, enjoy it, celebrate it, and thank him for it. Thank him for giving you the most miraculous means of all for hearing his voice.

"I am leaving you with a gift—peace of mind and heart. And the peace I give is a gift the world cannot give. So don't be troubled or afraid" (John 14:27).

The cardinal is a source of peace and comfort.

The cardinal continued to appear to my family on birthdates in such special ways. On Kristoffer's twelfth and thirteenth birthdays, a cardinal hovered in our backyard all afternoon on the freshly snow-covered trees. It was the most beautiful sight to see. It reminded us of the Badger Red Rose Bowl Kristoffer was able to celebrate in California as Matt's last trip the year before. Kristoffer's birthday is during the holidays, so his birthday was celebrated the previous year in California with Matt. The saying is that in times of celebration or despair, a cardinal will show up as a sign that your loved one is still with you.

Just days before my fortieth birthday, I received the best birthday gift ever. It was knocking at my front door. I went outside to see what was going on. To my surprise, I found a female cardinal swooping in with branches, building a nest on the beautiful red tulip wreath on my front door. I was in awe again and couldn't believe it! I had never seen a cardinal build a nest on a front door wreath. I saw the beautiful male in a tall nearby tree in the front of my yard, watching as the female built the nest. It was a very dreary day in early May, and the trees had just begun budding. I hadn't even seen many birds out and about yet. I knew the cardinal had shown up for my fortieth birthday. I was beyond elated. I got a gorgeous picture of the female sitting in her completed nest. It is so beautiful; it looks like it was designed as part of the wreath.

Male cardinal watching as female builds nest

I saved the nest on the wreath and still hang it on the front door every spring. I've been told by visitors how beautiful the nest is and asked if it's part of the original wreath. I'm excited when I get to share my amazing story.

One night when picking my son up from basketball, I felt a strong nudge from the Holy Spirit to tell Kristoffer's basketball coach, Tony, about the cardinal story. I knew he would enjoy it and receive my story well as he was a spiritual man. He signed his basketball-related emails with "God bless." I then had a voice inside my head tell me, "Sara, you don't need to share this story with everyone." I hesitated, but then a strong conviction from the Holy Spirit came to me again and asked me to share the story.

I approached Tony and told him my story. As I began, Dave, a dad I had never met, overheard and came closer to listen. As we walked out to our cars, Dave told me he loved my story and that he really appreciated my sharing it. I could tell he was really moved by it. Dave passed away unexpectedly just a couple of months later.

This had been my one and only interaction with him. I know now that was why I was prompted so strongly to share the story. It was meant primarily for Dave rather than for the coach.

We went to the funeral home with our condolences for Dave's family. At the visitation, I shared the story of the cardinal with his wife, Amy, and she said Dave had told her about it the evening he'd returned home from practice with their son, Evan, who played basketball with Kristoffer. Amy said Dave and Evan were touched by my story.

My husband and I went to the west side of Michigan for a weekend getaway to celebrate our fortieth birthdays. My mom came to stay at our house with the kids. We stayed at a bed and breakfast in Douglas, Michigan, and spent some time in Holland, Michigan, and Saugatuck, Michigan. As we shopped in the cute Saugatuck stores, my husband noticed a silver bird feather-shaped necklace. The tag on it read "a messenger from heaven to earth." We asked the owner, Wendy, if she had a bracelet or earrings with the feather.

We told her our story of the cardinal and how the feather sign, indicating a messenger from heaven, resonated with us through the cardinals that we saw after my brother had passed away. Wendy said her store was founded on the idea of the cardinal. She had an aunt and other relatives pass away so she saw cardinals often. Wendy said the red dot on her store logo is a little red bird that symbolizes the cardinal.

I showed Wendy the picture of the cardinal that built the nest on our front door, and she was blown away by the beauty of it. She showed us a little red cardinal that she has secured to the window frame of her store. Wendy explained that she randomly found it in the floor vent of her current store when cleaning up as she was turning what was a furniture store into a handcrafted jewelry store. She said she saw it as a sign from her aunt that she was doing the right thing opening this store.

Wendy uses some of the most beautiful gemstones found on earth for her pieces, gemstones with romantic histories, magical stories, and inspired beliefs. After first beginning with affirmations such as *ponder, grace, belief, courage,* and *gratitude,* Wendy then selects gemstones that resonate with the affirmation. The resulting jewelry pieces are imbued with a transcendent power and beauty that elevates them above ordinary body decorations.

8

These miraculous signs will accompany those who believe: They will cast out demons in my name, and they will speak in new languages.

—Mark 16:17

We are all connected.

The cardinal is a special symbol of my brother, Matthew. Everyone who knows me knows how much I love these birds. Many friends have given me special cardinal paintings or pieces for my home. They all hold a very intimate place in my heart, and I associate each one with the person who gave it to me.

I have spread my story through many on Facebook. One of my Facebook friends asked how my inspirational story about the cardinal was coming. At the time, I was chatting with another acquaintance, Beth. I briefly filled in Beth on what my book was about, and she told me that she lost her young adult sister and that she sees cardinals often. She thinks they are a sign from her sister. I told her the meaning of a cardinal, and she was so moved when she learned that they represent the afterlife.

Another friend lost her mother recently and knows my story. She and her sisters see cardinals all the time since the death of their mother. She has sent me pictures where it's perched on the top of a tall tree or on the peak of a rooftop. She says she and her sister have seen them while on a walk and when praying for wisdom. They know without a doubt that it is their mother.

I don't see cardinals now nearly as frequently as I had during the first year or two after Matt's death. When I do see one in a unique place, though, it is always associated with a special occasion. April 11, 2017, I drove my daughter Molly home from volleyball at 9:00 p.m. to see the cardinal in the same location by the garage where that first one had appeared before the first Christmas Matt had been gone. Molly took a video of it, since it wasn't afraid and wouldn't move at the sight of people. I showed the video to my other daughter Kaitlyn, and she said the cardinal came this week to wish me a happy birthday. We checked at 11:00 p.m. on Kaitlyn's twelfth birthday and it was there. It was also there on Easter night, April 16.

The summer of 2017, Kaitlyn's guinea pig was dying, and she insisted I drive it to the vet to see if there was something that could be done so that it wouldn't suffer. I drove and pulled over at the Harvestland Church, about a mile from our house, to call Kris. I wanted to tell him about the guinea pig's condition and get his thoughts on how long he thought it would take for it to pass away. As I was talking to Kris, I looked up and saw two cardinals hovering right in front of me in the woods. They were there the entire time until the guinea pig took its last breath. I could hardly believe they were present and God was right there during the death of the guinea pig.

This is a God who cares about all his creation and an all-knowing God who knows the details of his people, their pets, and their feelings. I am in awe when I think about how God has personally shown himself in so many ways through the cardinal.

On February 27, 2018, I pulled into my garage after dropping the kids off at school, and a red cardinal immediately flew into my garage and onto the hood of my vehicle. It pivoted around for about thirty seconds right in front of my eyes. I hadn't had a chance to even open my door. I thought, *What is the significance of this date?* I had never experienced this; was it trying to get my attention? I thought, *Well, it may be my grandfather.* He had passed away a month earlier. I couldn't think of any other significance to this date until I was on Facebook later that afternoon.

There was a post from Amy saying that it was her husband, John's, birthday. That was the man I mentioned earlier who was so interested in my cardinal story and then passed away just a few weeks later. It had been my only interaction with him. The cardinal appeared and spoke to me in such a unique way for John's birthday. Amy had asked on her Facebook post to share any stories or memories any of John's friends had about him. I shared the fact that the cardinal showed up on the hood of my car this morning on John's birthday. What a comfort for John's family and friends who read my post to experience the comfort of knowing John's eternal spirit lives on.

On John's birthday in 2020, I got a text from Amy saying that their son, Evan, texted her that morning from the University of Dayton to say that a cardinal literally just flew right in front of him. It was the first cardinal he had ever seen at school. *Dad is with me!* he said. God used me for a purpose in his nudge to share the cardinal story. God wanted Evan to hear it and witness a sign of God's love and faith to Evan during his first year of college. God uses his people to accomplish his purposes, so if you get a nudge from the Holy Spirit to speak, please don't ignore it!

May 2019 came all too soon. Kristoffer had many events leading to his high school graduation on June 3. He was a varsity basketball player who made it through a time that many division one athletes moved in and surrounded him in our district. Kristoffer has determination and grit. He spent endless hours practicing throughout the years. It was his determination and dedication to the sport that got him through the ups and downs of this journey.

Also, when final grades were released, Kristoffer was one of the top twenty-five scholars of his graduation class of around 650 students. His principal sent him a letter mentioning Kristoffer's grit to finish senior year strong and not give up when he thought no one was watching. He is a truly remarkable and kind soul who was given several cardinal signs as an honor to his accomplishments over his school years.

Kristoffer came home from work one day after school was finished for the senior students. He was looking at his phone, checking messages, and opened his car door to get some air. A female cardinal flew in and sat on his steering wheel for a brief moment and flew back out. Kristoffer was in awe but realized it was a specific sign and blessing from above congratulating him on his efforts and accomplishments.

My children have been completely moved throughout the years with the cardinal and how it appears to confirm that there is more to life than us. God has a plan and purpose for all of us, and he is sending specific signs of this to our family. What a blessing to have faith and eternal signs time and time again supporting it. God is magnificent and wondrous. He lives in each and every one of us if we are connected to him. He is the vine and we are the branches.

My husband found a cardinal nest in the bush right by our garage door where we first discovered the bird at night. He found it the week leading up to Kristoffer's graduation party. It had built it in the perfect place to be smack dab in the middle of the party festivities, between the party tent where the guests sat to eat and the deck tent where they approached to see Kristoffer's special awards and pictures and all the drinks and food. Every guest walked right past that bush with the cardinal's nest eggs. We originally wanted to set up the party tent in the backyard but weren't able to due to the excessive rain we had gotten all spring. We set up on the driveway, which was God's perfect plan for it.

We serve a truly amazing God who gives natural signs if we are open to them. We need to open our eyes and trust his goodness always, despite our circumstances. God is always, always good.

My dad passed away of pancreatic cancer in June 2020. I headed back to Appleton, Wisconsin, to see him as hospice told us it was time. The first thing I noticed as I entered his room at the assisted living facility was a beautiful framed bird puzzle hanging on his wall. It had male and female cardinals! Assisted living had framed it for him and hung it on his wall since it was the last puzzle he'd completed. To me this was another special sign of God's presence.

Throughout the years, the cardinal has had a profound impact of faith on my daughter, even though she was only in first grade when Matt passed away. She wrote her "I Believe" narrative in eighth grade for a class. She previously shared it with me as she asked me to find a picture of her with Matt to show when she presented it to the class.

Kaitlyn's "I Believe" Narrative

I believe that everything happens for a reason. I believe that God creates a plan for all of us. All my life I've been told that everything happens for a reason. I was always fascinated by the inspiring, sad and impossible things that happened to people. I always knew that everything happened for a reason, but I didn't understand this until I had experienced it.

Six years ago, my uncle died of brain cancer. I was seven years old. When this happened, my whole family was devastated. We also were disappointed at the fact that he was only thirty-two years old and had lost his life. We had no idea why this would happen to him at such a young age. He could have done many more things in life and made a positive impact on the world. This wasn't fair; he hadn't done anything to deserve losing his life. We quickly realized that if we didn't get past this, then we wouldn't be living life to its fullest potential.

At my uncle's funeral, my mom saw a cardinal flutter past her as she was visiting his grave. She said that she got the feeling it was a sign from God. The bright red reminded her of the Wisconsin red where she grew up. Since that moment, everywhere my mom went she would see cardinals, especially at our house. The cardinal would go to one spot on the tree by our house, even during the winter. We could get a few feet away from it and it wouldn't move. My uncle's spirit fed off the energy of the cardinal. My mom didn't think of it as a coincidence that my uncle had just died and she was seeing cardinals. She knew this sign was from God.

One time, my mom posted a picture of a cardinal on Facebook. Having no clue what the sign of seeing the cardinal was, my mom's friend told her that the cardinal is the sign of the afterlife. Every day after that we saw the cardinal as the representation of my uncle and that he was always here with us. It also showed us that my uncle had died in peace and was happy in heaven.

One day, my whole family heard knocking on the door. We all went to check who was there. As we opened the door, we saw a nest. A cardinal nest was sitting on our wreath. We knew right then and there that we had to protect the babies. We looked after the babies every second of our lives. The cardinal's eggs quickly hatched, causing the cardinal to leave in a hurry. The cardinal flew to a different and mysterious spot so we didn't get to see it as much.

We usually see the cardinal on important dates or in time of celebration; and when that time comes, we know it is a moment to cherish. Seeing this beautiful cardinal, we understand that it is my uncle's spirit and that God is showing us that my uncle is living.

God blessed our daughter Kaitlyn with a sign to help her understand faith deeply at a young age. My children were blessed to have experienced such visual signs and a story of faith when they were young.

Dear children, let's not merely say that we love each other; let us show the truth by our actions."

—1 John 3:18

I have placed my rainbow in the clouds. It is the sign of my covenant with you and with all the earth.

—Genesis 9:13

In a matter of a month in the winter of 2018, three friends had lost a parent. All three parents were seventy-nine years old when they passed. We had our friend Greg over to give him a garden stone in memory of his mother. We hadn't been able to make it to Traverse City for her funeral. Greg is a sarcoma cancer survivor. We happened to be talking and mentioned a friend of ours, Celeste, who was fighting pancreatic cancer.

Greg soon came to realize that he had just met her husband about a week earlier. Celeste's husband, Jared, is the school psychologist of Lake Orion schools and needed to go to court to confirm that Greg and his wife would still be legal guardians of their son, Greg, who had just turned eighteen and has special needs from a chromosomal defect.

Jared had told Greg of his wife, Celeste, having pancreatic

cancer. As we were discussing, Greg noticed a red cardinal on the bush right outside our front window. That led me to show Greg the red cardinal that Celeste had Jared's mom paint for me before she was diagnosed with cancer. Celeste was always touched by my story of the cardinal and how it appeared to me after my brother's death. She was so thoughtful to have her mother-in-law paint such a special gift (pictured on the cover of this book). It now hangs in my kitchen.

When my forty-four-year-old friend Celeste was diagnosed with pancreatic cancer in June 2017, I gave her a *Jesus Is Calling* book to give her a small passage to read each day to encourage her along her unknown journey and to help her keep her eyes on God. I was arranging a day to give her the book and pay her a visit since I hadn't seen her in person since the diagnosis. The morning of July 29 I sent her a text asking if she felt well enough for me to stop by. I decided to read the *Jesus Is Calling* message for that day to read in advance what it would be saying to Celeste. It read,

> Come to me continually. I am means to be the Center of your consciousness. The Anchor of your soul. Your mind will wander from me, but the question is how far you allow it to wander. An anchor on a short rope lets a boat drift only slightly before the taut line tugs the boat back toward the center. Similarly, as you drift away from me, my spirit within you gives a tug, prompting you to return to me. As you become increasingly attuned to my presence, the length of the rope on your soul's anchor is shortened. You wander only a short distance before feeling that inner tug, telling you to return to your true center in me. (https://www.midlandscbd.com/articles/jesus-calling-july-29-16283)

I knew this was God speaking directly to Celeste, and this was a sign that this book was meant for her. Celeste and I share a love of anchors. I gave her an anchor ornament the Christmas before she was diagnosed. She has them all over her house, and we both love the water. I have loved all things nautical, as well as boating and the lake, since I was a teenager.

Celeste sent me a picture of this message from the *Jesus Is Calling* book in July 2018, a year after I gave it to her. She was thanking me for the book and that the messages were so helpful to her throughout the year. She said this is the message it all began with. I needed that message just at that time and had forgotten what a beautiful image it is of our relationship with God and the anchor.

God is right on time. He speaks to us through people, friends, nature, and other ways. That message on July 29 from *Jesus Is Calling* came back full circle a year later when I needed this reminder the most. I thought, *May I keep this message close at heart not only through rough waters but through smooth sailing as well.*

Another time, a woman came to my door to purchase gymnastics leotards we were selling through a mom-to-mom sale site. She was a stranger who mentioned being a nurse in the ICU and often saw people pass away. I told her about my brother and the cardinals. She knew about the cardinals as a sign and proceeded to tell me that her neighbors had lost their fifteen-year-old son to leukemia. She said they traveled away the first Christmas he was gone since the memories at home were too painful without him. She said she witnessed a rainbow almost every day over the neighbors' house while they were away. She even showed me a picture, having taken it for the parents while they were away. God was showing his presence and protection of the family through this sign of the rainbow. This woman and I shared tears together over these signs and the death of these young people even though we only shared ten minutes of our time together and hadn't ever met before. After she left, I was reading the book *Parenting the Wholehearted Child* and immediately read about the sign of a rainbow.

I attended a Bible study called The Armor of God, by Priscilla Shirer, at the Clarkston United Methodist Church. One week, a woman named Laura, who opened a coffee shop in the church for fellowship, was there. She'd hoped that children from nearby schools would have a safe place to come to do homework and meet with friends for warm drinks. She told us of God giving her a vision to open this coffee shop ministry. She talked to her pastor about it, and he had a similar thought. He said that if more than one person has the same idea in the church, then this is a confirmation it is from God.

Laura wanted to confirm that God was the one behind this meeting place rather than it being her own idea. She talked to family, and her son, Matt's, girlfriend, Makayla, of seven years loved the idea and wanted to help open up and run this shop. Laura got tears in her eyes as she told that soon after, Makayla died in a car accident on her way to work in Ann Arbor. Laura said that the planned date for her coffee shop to open was the same as Makayla's birthday. Her saying this brought tears to my eyes. I felt that this was definitely a sign from God as I had experience with dates as signs. Laura explained how it being Makalya's birthday was a confirmation of God wanting this coffee shop.

Laura said we should come during our break to enjoy a cup of coffee. I took her up on her offer and talked to Laura about my brother and how his death, funeral, and burial fell on family members' birthdates. I told her about how I was touched by that and by her coffee shop opening date being Makalya's birthday. Laura proceeded to show me the heart on top of the sign for her shop, Front Porch Coffee, being a sign of Makalya.

She also showed me the sign of Front Porch Coffee ministry offering beverages and light snacks for all who visit the facility. In honor of a very special person, who will be remembered with each cup poured, this prayer is said: "May the coffee that is poured

here connect us to the community. May we see with God's eyes and hear with God's ears the needs of people and respond with Christ's love. May the grace of God be received with each cup.

"Taste and see that the Lord is good" (Psalm 34:8).

Laura asked me to bring in a picture of the cardinal nest wreath on my front door so she could display it in her coffee shop since this is what the coffee shop is all about.

I told her I knew of the story of Makayla since at the time of the funeral, a friend asked if I could take her daughter home after the half day of school as she would be attending the funeral for Makayla who went to high school with her daughter.

I then asked Laura how her son was doing. She said he was a baseball pitcher and that he had some major league opportunities, but the loss of Makayla had set him back. He turned to helping to train pitchers. I told her Kristoffer's best friend since kindergarten, Mason, was a left-handed pitcher who may know him. She said she thought Mason would know her son, Matt. Mason sure did and had been trained by him. In fewer than fifteen minutes of talking, we made so many connections.

Coincidence? Absolutely not. We are all truly connected. We just have to stop and realize things aren't a coincidence but just part of the connection we have through God. God is everywhere. He is above us, below us, and all around every one of us. There is no place he is not. If you are having trouble seeing God, please ask him to open the eyes of your heart so that you can "see" his presence. This is a prayer that God loves to hear and answer.

For I can do everything through Christ, who
gives me strength.

—Philippians 4:13

Suffering is ultimately part of God's exalted purposes and is
always under his perfect, sovereign care. God may allow
suffering to awaken our spirits. Sometimes, God allows suffering
so he and his work can be revealed.

The believer can be assured God loves and cares for his
people. He sent Jesus, his son, into the world to live as we live
and to suffer and die for us. God refused to remove the thorn of
suffering from apostle Paul so that God's grace might be seen and
proven sufficient. Though no one would choose hardships, there
is no greater proof of God's power and grace than when he gives
a person supernatural strength within the pain. Often this brings
even greater impact from God than would a miraculous healing.

"Even before he made the world, God loved us and chose us
in Christ to be holy and without fault in his eyes" (Ephesians 1:4).

Love overcomes pain and fear of a terminal illness. Part of
God's plan was for my sister-in-law, Melissa, to take care of Matt
and be his wife during such a difficult time.

"For I know the plans I have for you," says the Lord. "They
are plans for good and not for disaster, to give you a future and a
hope" (Jeremiah 29:11).

We go through exactly what Christ goes through. If we go through the hard times with him, then we certainly will go through the good times with him.

"Love is the simple truth that continues to weave itself into the tapestry of every great story" (*Love Does* by Bob Goff).

Melissa was sent by God as an angel to display God's love, care, and kindness to my brother, Matt. A girlfriend of only eight months before the brain tumor was revealed, yet she decided to stay, to marry Matt, and to be by his side until death did they part. This is real agape love—the highest form of love, charity, and the love of God for man and of man for God. It is a universal, unconditional love that transcends and persists regardless of circumstances.

Melissa was only in her twenties and was sent through marriage, death, and tons of life lessons at an early age. I remember her mom saying she had a feeling of not being able to move on after Matt died, which is completely understandable. She had a broken heart that went through so much, and she needed time to heal.

My aunt, Kathy, passed away of breast cancer a couple of years before Matt died. She gifted some of her money to her nieces and nephews as she didn't have any children of her own and never married. Melissa was able to use this money after Matt passed away to go on vacations, take time off of work, and do many yoga retreats, which aided in her healing process.

Melissa found it too difficult with all the memories associated with Chicago to stay there. She decided to move to California to start anew. Soon after, she met her current husband, who helped comfort and console her throughout her heart-healing process. The emotional connection developed between them, and they were married and now have two sons. Melissa was remarried on Kris's and my anniversary. I think this is another important date sign. Kris was Matt's best man in his wedding, and Matt had a brotherly love for Kris.

God had a purpose in Chicago for Melissa, and she was faithful to God's calling and served him even though it was so painful and difficult for her. God restored her broken heart and had a plan to bless her with another husband and two sons.

The end is just the beginning.